THE YELLOW LEGACIES

THE YELLOW LEGACIES

Danica Hobbs

authorHOUSE®

AuthorHouse™
1663 Liberty Drive
Bloomington, IN 47403
www.authorhouse.com
Phone: 1-800-839-8640

© 2013 by Danica Hobbs. All rights reserved.

No part of this book may be reproduced, stored in a retrieval system, or transmitted by any means without the written permission of the author.

Published by AuthorHouse   01/14/2013

ISBN: 978-1-4685-8008-2 (sc)
ISBN: 978-1-4685-8007-5 (e)

Library of Congress Control Number: 2012906273

Any people depicted in stock imagery provided by Thinkstock are models, and such images are being used for illustrative purposes only.
Certain stock imagery © Thinkstock.

This book is printed on acid-free paper.

Because of the dynamic nature of the Internet, any web addresses or links contained in this book may have changed since publication and may no longer be valid. The views expressed in this work are solely those of the author and do not necessarily reflect the views of the publisher, and the publisher hereby disclaims any responsibility for them.

Part I
1978

"Ma, my bus is going to be leavin' in a few. All you have to do is call and tell them you talked to me and I changed my mind," said Kelvin reluctantly.

"Hell no!" she yelled. "You was tryin' to be smart when you went and signed up, tryin' to hurt us, but now you scared," his mother replied. "So you take your ass on and go!"

Kelvin, with a look of frustration for his mother, quietly got into the car where his twin brother, Keith, and eldest brother, Charles, were waiting to take him to his recruitment destination. Just as Keith had started to pull off from the big yellow house with the blue fire hydrant in front of it, he remembered that in all the drama of the day's events he hadn't got a chance to say good-bye to his sisters, Karen and Denise. "Stop for a minute!" he yells at Keith, sitting in the driver's seat. "I gotta say bye to Sly and Dee." Sly (Karen) and Dee (Denise) were the nicknames Kelvin and Keith had given their sisters when they were little, and those names stuck with them far beyond their youth. Now young adults, they were plagued by the names their brothers adorned them with. "Sly!" yelled Kelvin. "Dee!" he screamed. "I'm leavin'!"

As Karen and Denise came running out the front door and down the steps, they noticed their mother sitting on the banister with her arms folded, coldly staring at them as they ran past. "You all take care. I am going to miss y'all most," Kelvin said as he hugged them both at the same time.

"You make sure you bring me back a tall dark man in uniform now!" Dee joked. Being the baby sister, she had one thing on her mind more than the older sister—men!

"Make sure you don't get shot!" Sly said worriedly. Sly had always had a more serious disposition than Dee, which made her a bit more uptight at times than all the other siblings.

"Bye, Sly," said Kelvin as he rolled his eyes and got in the car finally. As they pulled off, Kelvin thought about one last good-bye to say, and that would be to his dad. He was working a swing shift at the mill. Kelvin would call him when he got to his destination the following day. "Keith and Charles," said Kelvin, "make sure you tell Dad to take it easy!"

Kelvin's mother, Shirley Ann, came from broken beginnings, and the pieces would never really be put together. Shirley Ann never knew her mother and father and was juggled from one aunt and uncle to another, from New Jersey to Kentucky and many points between. She was never given the chance in her youth to have a normal family life and develop a sensible feeling of family pride. The last thing Shirley Ann wanted when she started her own family was to feel the abandonment of her youth again, so she decided to clutch tight that which she held most dear—her family. So when it was time to finally develop her own family, she vowed to keep them close together by whatever means necessary. Usually her ends did not justify the means, but could Shirley Ann really be held accountable for her way of doing things? It was her past experiences in her life that scarred her anyway.

One of the best things that had happened in Shirley Ann's life was meeting Ronnie, her husband of almost thirty years. Although a hardworking man, Ronnie had his moments of instability. He had learned at a young, tender age to play the sax like no one's business. This brought him much acclaim, both locally and nationally. Unfortunately this brought Shirley Ann much heartbreak and dismay at times. Ronnie was somewhat sought after by women because of his playing in several bands in his younger years. In his travels he was even rumored to have played with people like B. B. King and backed up Ray Charles.

Ronnie had become quite the ladies' man. He developed a reputation with the women. Ronnie always tried to hide his moments of infidelity, but it somehow continuously crept up into Shirley Ann's and Ronnie's relationship. Therefore, Shirley Ann decided to live the method of "see no evil, hear no evil." She internally suppressed all of her fears of Ronnie's unfaithfulness and developed a "what you don't see won't hurt you" attitude. So when it was time for Ronnie to go on the road with the band and for Shirley Ann to stay at home with the children, she would seem unmoved by his calls telling her he would be home "later than expected." After a while she learned how to be without Ronnie and take care of the children on her own, seldom harboring any thoughts at all about Ronnie's probable indiscretions. How relieved Shirley Ann was when his career slow down and he took a job at the local steel mill in 1964. Ronnie worked for $2.50 an hour on a twelve-hour swing shift, but he still found time in between to play the sax with one of his bands every now and again. Although he never found the acclaim to make him world famous, he became much like a local celebrity in his own right.

In addition to Ronnie's and Shirley Ann's marital moments of discontent, they both were still in the process of trying to find their way after a tragedy like no other. Ronnie and Shirley Ann's union saw the births of the Brady Bunch (three boys and three girls). However, two years earlier their eldest daughter Ronnell, named after Ronnie, lost her life in a motor vehicle accident. Years later, Shirley Ann and Ronnie were trying to cope with altered dynamics of their family.

Ronnell, the eldest daughter, was gone forever and taken her very essence with her. Ronnell was intelligent and strong in many ways, and Shirley Ann had found her strength refreshing and much needed as the eldest. Ronnell had also left behind two daughters who were infants and toddlers when she passed away. Shirley Ann and Ronnie jumped directly into the role of parents in their grandchildren's lives, and so their commitment to Ronnell in life was just as much concentrated on in her tragic death. Shirley Ann and Ronnie's life was to be always dedicated to the lives of the two children Ronnell had reared until her end.

Part 2
1980

"Is it almost time?" said Denise.

"Calm down," said Karen.

"What do you mean, calm down? I'm getting married in forty-five minutes!"

"I mean try to stay as calm as possible," replied Karen. "Everything will go fine. Don't put all your emphasis on the wedding, put *all* your emphasis on the *man*!"

"That might be one of your best ideas ever." Denise smiled. "So how's Ma doing?"

"I don't even have to tell you. You know that Ma is Ma!" Karen said, shrugging.

"So I can just about take from that statement she is still not happy about me getting married!" Denise exclaimed. As Karen went and got her veil from the closet in the bedroom, Denise wondered how her parents, Shirley Ann and Ronnie, would deal with her upcoming marriage. Of course she understood the dynamics of her parents' issues when it came to her moving away and going to live on base with her husband-to-be in Germany. He was a sergeant in the Air Force. Denise had never been away from home and really never wanted to be. She was a retail sales manager with one of the local department stores and planned on becoming head manager soon. She was very strong-willed in her own right, much like her mother and eldest sister. Denise had developed a sense of independence as well as a free spirit.

She was still entranced in thought when Karen said, "Lets go—it's almost time to walk down the aisle!"

The wedding had been very last-minute, so instead of a church wedding Denise had settled for a small house wedding. Anthony, her groom-to-be, was to ship out three days after the wedding, but Denise could not join him until three months later. Soon they would move to Germany and live on base. There, they would begin their life together and live happily ever after.

Downstairs, all the immediate family and first cousins were gathered to see the union of Anthony and Denise. The big yellow house with the blue fire hydrant in front was beautifully decorated with streamers and bells and with blue and white balloons fitting for the occasion. To Denise's surprise, everything had come together beautifully, thanks to Karen and *some* members of the family.

"Denise it's time to meet your man downstairs!" Karen said excitedly. As Denise proceeded out of the room that she and her sisters had shared for so many years, she found herself a little sentimental, which was unusual for her. "Well, this is the last time I'll be in this room with you," she said.

"Yeah, I know," said Karen. As they walked out of the room and down the hallway to the top of the stairs, they embraced each other and smiled lovingly.

Back downstairs, at the end of the aisle stood Anthony, the groom, alongside Keith and Charles. To Anthony's right stood Shirley Ann and Ronnie, who had waited until the very last minute to come down and stand in the wedding party. No one knew where the bad blood between

Shirley Ann and Anthony had come from, but it was definitely still there on Anthony's and Denise's special day.

Shirley Ann, once again in her nonchalant way, made it very clear she would rather be cooking Sunday dinner and preparing her famous dressing, the way she did on every other Saturday afternoon, than standing here doing this. Her fidgeting and sighing were a dead giveaway for everyone to see. Her youngest daughter was leaving her in three months, and Shirley Ann felt as she always had when faced with situations of this magnitude. She once again believed the family was in danger of breaking up.

Ronnie, on the other hand, had more of an "I'll play along" attitude when it came to Anthony. He was a very blunt man, and beating around the bush was not in his character. In most situations he showed restraint until pushed. Ronnie also had a soft spot in his heart for Denise, his baby girl, so he would bend a little more than Shirley Ann when it came to Denise. Shirley Ann and Denise had an oil and water relationship at times and seldom mixed. Although their mother and daughter relationship was strained, they still found common ground in some things.

As the music began, Karen, slender and tall, came down the steps in her high-necked baby blue lace bridesmaid's gown, carrying a light blue bouquet in her hands fitting for a maid of honor. As soon as Karen got to the end of the aisle, Denise started her descent. Denise was adorned in a traditional wedding gown with white-on-white lace trim from the neck down and small embroidered beads placed strategically all over.

Anthony stood awestruck at the sight of Denise as she came down the aisle. He slowly bent over with a smile and whispered between his teeth to Shirley Ann, "I guess I won!"

She replied in the same hissing tone, "You may have won the battle, ass, but you have not won the war!" And the ceremony began.

Part 3
1982

*K*AREN, THE MIDDLE daughter of Shirley Ann and Ronnie, was in her early twenties. She had been living at home because that was what she thought her parents wanted and needed. She was the kind of person who tried to please everyone no matter what the cost to herself. She demanded little effort from everyone when it concerned herself and would all but give the shirt off her back if it pleased everyone else. Being so easygoing cost Karen a lot of time and energy in most of her circumstances, and she knew it.

Karen had two children several years apart, mainly because she followed her heart rather than her head. She was a hopeless romantic and never stopped believing in Prince Charming. She was a daydreamer and often thought about her "knight in shining armor" coming to whisk her away from the occasional extreme hold of Shirley Ann and Ronnie.

Compared to the other siblings, Karen was different in so many ways. In several ways she stood out physically because she was the tallest in the family with the exception of Charles, her older brother. She was very thin and somewhat ungraceful at times. Karen's book smarts were second to none, but her street smarts would need a little help at times. To her siblings, this made her a bit naïve because they felt like they needed to protect her more than any other brother or sister.

Karen also had many talents that she developed over the years.

One day as Ronnie was coming downstairs he heard music playing in the basement. He crept to the basement stairs slowly and looked down to see what was playing. Maybe a tape or radio, he thought. It was the sound of a solo saxophone. Accompanying the saxophone was a band playing in the background; however, the lead was the saxophone itself. Ronnie kept inching down the stairs to get a closer look of what was actually going on. To Ronnie's surprise he saw Karen playing the saxophone like no one's business. "Karen!" he yelled.

"Yes, Dad," she answered, startled, putting the saxophone down hurriedly.

"What the hell are you doing with my saxophone?" he asked.

Karen replied, "I'm just playing. I've been playing for at least six years now. I love the saxophone, just like you, Dad. It's like I have the same gift. I learned to play by ear and now I can pick up almost anything!"

Ronnie replied, "As long as I live I better not even catch your little narrow behind on the saxophone! It's not very nice for a woman to play the sax!"

Karen, deflated, said, "But I love the saxophone, and I was hoping you and I could play together soon."

Ronnie replied, "Are you crazy, Karen? A woman should know her place, and it ain't in the club with me playing the damn saxophone."

"But Dad!" Karen pleaded.

"No buts, Karen. Now that's the end of this conversation. Put my saxophone up, and don't touch it again!"

Karen put the saxophone back in the case and decided never to pick it up again . . . forever.

Part 4
1984

*C*HARLES, THE ELDEST boy, was a mild-mannered young man. He was very quiet but charming. He dedicated his life to Shirley Ann and Ronnie. He was the model son for any parent to have. He was soft-spoken but confident and extremely intelligent.

Staying inside his room mostly, Charles would read in his encyclopedias for hours on end and pore over any other books he could get his hands on. To some this made Charles seem awkward because he would rather read than go to a club and chase women. Unlike his younger twin brothers Kelvin and Keith, he showed more restraint when it came to the ladies. He would often get stuck in the "friend zone" when it came to most women. He had nice but average looks, but his personality won people over through and through.

He also had a very special relationship with Karen's and Ronnell's children. He was the only father figure they had ever known. He adored his nieces and nephews, and they adored him. His sense of humor made the children feel as though he was one of them. He took them many places like parades, parks, and movies. They deemed him the wisest man in the world because no matter what question they asked of him, he knew the answer immediately.

One of Charles's wishes was that one day he would have a family and children of his own also.

Charles worked at the mill with his father, just for the lack of not quite finding anything better, for a little more than five dollars an hour. Now the million dollar question around was, as bright as he was, why didn't he pursue a college career or any type of higher education? It was often said that Charles tried to please Ronnie and Shirley Ann so much he put off his life's desires to please his parents. Being mild-mannered and soft-spoken, sometimes he could be mistaken as passive, and knowing this, his parents could be a bit persuasive in their ways.

"Charles," Shirley Ann yelled. "What are you doing?"

"Ma, I'm looking through the newspaper," he said.

"For what?"

"I'm thinking about finally moving out and getting my own place," Charles said.

"Why are you doing that?" she asked, surprised.

"Ma, I'm almost in my mid-thirties, and it has been past time to go out on my own and get my own place!"

"Have you lost your mind?" cried Shirley Ann. "You got a roof over your head and food to eat! The only thing your dad and I won't let you have is those fast-behind girls in here, and now you ready to leave us."

"Ma!" he said. "When have I ever asked to have fast-behind girls here?" He chuckled, seeing that his mother was being a little condescending.

"Are you trying to be a smart-ass?" she asked. "You ain't too old for me to kick your behind till it rots like okra!" Shirley Ann always had little sayings for every occasion.

"Ma, I just was thinking about it," Charles said.

"Well, don't think too damn hard!" Shirley said. "Dinner is almost ready now. Come eat."

Part 5
1986

Although Kelvin and Keith were identical twins, they were opposites in every way. Sometimes they would be at odds with each other because they were so much alike and couldn't see it. At times they were in steep competition with each other about everything. They both possessed a spirit of rebellion—even to a point of self-destruction. They were very handsome young men and well built.

If there was one thing that Kelvin and Keith excelled at, that would be getting into mischief. Although Charles, being the oldest, served as a perfect role model for his younger brothers, they decided not to follow in his footsteps and to make their own way. Everything to the twins was like a game, even the young ladies they would come across. When one twin got tired of a girl, the other would pretend to be his twin brother and continue on with the relationship until he got tired.

Kelvin and Keith were star athletes in high school, so they were fit. Kelvin played basketball, and Keith played football. They were the envy of most jocks, and they ate it up because they craved the attention that came with being athletic and popular.

Kelvin was older than Keith by three and a half minutes, but you could rarely tell. Keith was the one who took care of Kelvin. He was the one who would tell Kelvin who, what, when, where, and why. He taught Kelvin everything. He more or less showed Kelvin the ropes—not always with positive reinforcement, but this was what brothers, especially twins, did to look out for one another regardless.

Now Kelvin had gone into the service years earlier. Keith had tried to talk him out of it, but Kelvin had such a strong-will to go out on his own that he hastily enlisted and then decided there were possibly other outlets he could have used to break what he felt were the strongholds of Shirley Ann and Ronnie. Although Keith was without his older twin, he still tried to maintain their "reps" back at home, even if it meant living a somewhat reckless youthful life forever.

One thing that was unique about the men in this particular family is that all four of their birthdays fell in the space of three days. June 28, 29, and 30 were covered every year with birthdays. So every year Shirley Ann, Karen, and Dee would often throw them one big birthday party to celebrate all together. All the first cousins and distant relatives would join in and come from everywhere to the birthday bash. Even distant family from other states would be in attendance.

"Hey, y'all," said Keith. "This party is it! Y'all throw us a good party every year," he said, while holding a cigarette in one hand and taking a sip of beer with the other.

"Yeah, this party is real nice!" said one of his cousins from out of town. Now this cousin was like a sibling to Keith because Shirley Ann and Ronnie had taken him in for many years when he was younger.

Shirley Ann and Ronnie were very strict. Still, secondary family as well as their children's friends would come to stay with them whenever they were going through a tough time. People often joked about the reason why everyone would flock to Shirley Ann and Ronnie's home. The inside joke was that with so many people already staying in the big yellow house with the blue fire hydrant, no one would know the difference with a couple of extra mouths to feed!

"Hey, Keith," said his cousin, "I just bought me a brand new candy-apple red Porsche last Friday after I got a promotion on my job. Would you like to see it?"

"Man you know I would love to see it," Keith said ecstatically.

"Where y'all going?" Ronnie asked as they headed up the basement stairs and out the back door.

"We'll be right back, Dad!" Keith said. They went around to the front of the house to examine the Porsche.

As they approached the candy-apple red Porsche, Keith yelled, "Ah, hell! Look at it!" Now to Keith, it was not just the most beautiful car he had ever laid his eyes on, but it represented a status symbol to him. To Keith, this car crossed all social barriers; it was exactly what he dreamed about all his life. His life could not get any better than this, he believed. "Hey cousin! Let's ride!"

"Sure!" his cousin said. As they got into the car, Keith looked around inside, reclined his seat all the way back, and dreamed away.

After riding around the city for about a half-hour, they arrived back at the house to continue enjoying the birthday party. As Keith got out of the car, he said, "Man, that is a bad ride!"

His cousin replied, "I know, that's why I bought it."

Keith came up with what he believed to be a wonderful idea. He thought that after they went back into the party, he would tell his cousin that he'd left his wallet in the car and ask for the keys to unlock the doors, Then he would take the car for a joyride without his cousin's knowledge and bring it right back.

Fifteen minutes after they had come back to the party, Keith decided to put his plan into action. He approached his cousin when he was preoccupied and said, "Man, I left my wallet in your car. Can I unlock your doors and get it?"

"Sure!" said his cousin, who was totally unaware of what was taking place.

"Thanks, man." Keith grabbed the keys out of his cousin's hand and started back up the steps to the back door. As he walked from around the back of the house and started toward the Porsche, he felt a kind of freedom as if this was going to change his life or something. It was funny. Why would he get such a rush from driving this Porsche? As he got into the car and started it, he chuckled and took off from in front of the yellow house with the blue fire hydrant.

Back inside the house, the party was still going strong. Everyone was partying and dancing to Luther Vandross and Bobby Blue Bland. At about 3 o'clock, Keith's cousin from out of town thought to himself that it was weird that he hadn't seen Keith for several hours since he had given him the keys to the Porsche. As Shirley Ann walked by, he tugged at her shirt and said, "Have you seen Keith?"

"No!" she said. "Why?" He explained to her that he hadn't seen Keith since they had came back from their joyride at about 12:30 a.m. and Keith told him he left his wallet in the car and was going out to get it. Shirley Ann right then and there, knowing her son, became almost petrified. "You so stupid!" she yelled out.

She'd no sooner got the words out of her mouth than Ronnie came charging down the stairs. "Shirley, the police officer is on the phone. He said Keith was in an awful accident and they don't think he's gonna make it!"

Part 6
1988

*D*ENISE'S MARRIAGE EIGHT years earlier failed after only six short months. She never made it to Germany to live on base with him because of his unfaithful nature. It came to be more than she could bear just after they were married. An annulment was filed shortly thereafter, and they soon parted and went their separate ways.

Several years passed, and she went on with her life, but she never really found her one and only true love—that is, until she came upon one of the—handsomest men in the world, Sam. He was exactly what she had been dreaming of since she was a little girl. They hit it off quickly and started a very serious relationship. To Denise, Sam was definitely "the one." He would do things like buy Denise her favorite stuffed animals and spray them with his cologne so she would think of him and only him. He took her places she had ever been.

As the relationship went on, they started contemplating marriage. Sam and Denise decided that although they were thinking about marriage, they would try to just cherish each moment as it came.

Sam, although handsome and smart, had his own reputation at times to deal with. He loved the ladies and the ladies loved him, so most would say. Although he at times could be a little free when it came to the women, that all changed when he met Denise. Along with this he was rumored to have a bigger problem: dabbling in narcotics. Still, it was only *rumored* to be true. So Denise didn't take it to heart because no one knew anything for sure.

One day Denise called Sam on the telephone and explained to him she believed she was possibly pregnant, to the surprise of them both. They had not really anticipated having children at this point in time. Denise, now twenty-eight years of age, was what some considered an "old maid." She waited later in life to have her children, unlike her sisters Ronnell and Karen, who had children in their early twenties. Although Sam and Denise were surprised, they decided there was no other choice but to welcome the baby with open arms.

Several months went by, and Denise at this time was about seven and a half months pregnant. She came home from work one day very concerned. She had been calling Sam all day and she hadn't heard from him. At first she just thought he was gone all day and had not received any of her calls. Later in the afternoon she tried calling his parents' house, but they had not heard from him since early that morning.

Denise sat down to eat something. She decided to turn on the television and watch a show until Sam called her. As she was flipping through the stations, she noticed the local news report. It was about 6 p.m., and she hadn't seen the early afternoon report. As she listened, the anchor said, "Good afternoon, this is Cheryl King with 21 Action News. Our lead story tonight is that police are now investigating a double homicide on the city's south side. Two men were found shot in an abandoned house, and police would give no further information." As Denise leaned closer to the television, she noticed the body they were covering up was that of her fiancé, Sam.

Part 7
1990

*K*ELVIN, WHO HAD been away from home for several years, decided to come for a visit. He was excited about bringing home his girlfriend of the last several months. He had been gone for so long that he felt a little anxious to be visiting his family. As excited as he was about seeing everyone, he was also very nervous.

He decided to leave out one small detail about the new love in his life when he talked with his parents, Shirley Ann and Ronnie. He thought it would be in everyone's best interest not to tell them that his girlfriend, Linda, was Caucasian. Kelvin felt like he was in love, and since he loved her, everyone else would feel the same way.

As their cab pulled up in front of the yellow house with the blue fire hydrant, Kelvin looked around and noticed it hadn't changed that much. He remembered the day he left, years earlier, and the events surrounding that day.

He had signed up for the armed services to escape what he believed were the strongholds of Shirley Ann and Ronnie. When he tried to get out on his own, they would not allow him because they said he was not ready yet. They had forbidden any talk of moving out. Therefore, Kelvin felt like he had no other choice but to enlist in the armed services as a way out.

At the time Kelvin enlisted, he was to swear in twice. Kelvin was told this by his enlistment officer. The first time he would swear in, when he took his physical, was just procedural, so if he wanted to pull out then and there he could, with his parents' objections, right up until the second swearing-in, which was the real thing. Therefore, the saga started when Kelvin decided, before the second swearing-in service, to rescind. All he needed to do for that to be accomplished was to get permission from his parents.

He went to Shirley Ann and Ronnie the day before he had his second swearing-in service. He stated to them that he believed he made a mistake and requested their help to keep him out of the armed services. Shirley Ann knew this was exactly the type of leverage she had been waiting for. She decided that since Kelvin had signed up and openly disregarded the unspoken family rule of never leaving the nest, she refused to sign for him to be discharged. Unfortunately, when Shirley Ann made a decision out of spite or anger, Ronnie always sided with her decision, no matter how erratic it might be.

Kelvin soon decided to stop procrastinating and step out of the cab with Linda at his side. As the cabdriver opened up the trunk to get their luggage out, Kelvin took a deep breath and started toward the yellow house. As he and Linda came onto the porch, out came Ronnie and Shirley Ann.

"Hey, Mom and Dad!" Kelvin said. "I want you to meet the love of my life. Say hello, all, to Linda."

Linda came from behind Kelvin and said, "Hello. Nice to meet you!"

The disbelief and shock on Shirley Ann's and Ronnie's faces told the whole story and then some. "Nice to meet you too, Linda," they replied. "Why don't you come in and eat something?" Shirley Ann said graciously as they walked into the house.

Part 8
1992

*K*EITH HAD SURVIVED a car wreck several years earlier, and after about a year of therapy he was back on his feet. Keith at this point in his life was in his early thirties and decided to try to settle down and make a stable life for himself. He would make the best of the situation and marry his longtime girlfriend Rita. They already had one child and one on the way.

Before Rita met Keith, she was well on her way to starting a career in business management. She had put herself through college and was completing her last year. She was a very attractive woman with a very proper accent that stood out. However, her whole persona changed after she met Keith. Rita believed that if she could conform to what Keith wanted her to be, they would be okay. This naïve belief of Rita turned out not to be so.

Keith discovered that somehow in their relationship, if Rita wanted to conform to his way of life, it would be okay with him. He would not try to stop her. Being very much like Shirley Ann, he put his talent for being persuasive in gear when it came to Rita. He knew exactly how to get to her and get his way. After a while, even Rita's appearance was different, as well as what she stood for and who she was.

The day of the wedding in itself was pure hysteria.

The cousin from out of town (whose Porsche Keith had wrecked years earlier) had come with his girlfriend to attend the private ceremony at the yellow house. She had some exotic name that everyone had a hard time pronouncing. She was a very beautiful woman who had been born and raised in Africa and moved to the States in the last ten years or so.

Now the problem was that she became extremely upset with her boyfriend (the cousin) for bringing her to meet his family without being engaged themselves. She decided not to play his game anymore and stop waiting on him to propose to her. Instead, she would take matters into her own hands on this evening. The plan she concocted was to hit on every man at the wedding who would pay her some attention. And she did!

Now everything was set. The yellow house was decorated beautifully for Keith's and Rita's wedding. It was the beginning of December, so festive colors were appropriate. Red and white bows and flowers adorned the living room and den where the wedding was set to take place. The furniture in the rooms had been removed and chairs the spectators set up, also adorned with the same red and white theme. Outside the house there were minimal decorations; because of the cold they really wouldn't stay put.

Although Rita was two months pregnant, she barely showed. She looked marvelous in her beaded white satin off-the-shoulder gown. Keith was very handsome as well in his white tuxedo with a red cummerbund and tie to match. The ceremony was beautiful and went off without a hitch.

After the ceremony was when the problem came into play.

As Charles walked down the steps from the upper level of the house, he ran into the girlfriend of the out-of-town cousin. "Hey, Charles, where you going in such a hurry?" she said.

"Oh, I'm just going back down to the reception to join the party."

"We could have a lot more fun up here!" she said.

Charles, being always the gentleman, thought she was joking and with his charm simply dismissed her suggestion. "I'll go and see if I can find Cousin for you, okay?"

"Whatever!" she said, waving him off, and walked away.

Keith had to step outside to take a breather at one point in the evening. He could barely believe he was married. On top of his nervousness and excitement, he had indulged in a little too much wine just to make it through the evening. As he took a second to collect his thoughts outside on the porch, his cousin's girlfriend came right out behind him and put her arms around him. "Whatcha doing?" she purred.

"I'm just taking five," he replied. He grabbed her hands and unwrapped them from around his waist with an awkward giggle.

"You don't look too happy about being married. You supposed to be in there with your beautiful bride!"

Keith looked at her suspiciously, walked up close, and said to her, "Oh, I'm very happy about my beautiful bride."

Just as he was in the middle of telling her what he really thought about her loose ways, his cousin came outside and said, "Hey what's going on here?"

Keith replied, "Man, I think you and your woman should have a long talk."

"I don't want to talk to him!" she replied.

The cousin replied to her, "Why are you acting like such a bitch since we came here?"

She screamed, "Because I hate you!"

Keith and his cousin were in utter shock and amazement. At that moment Keith's cousin, enraged by what had just came out of her mouth grabbed her by her hair and pulled her down off the porch. As Keith saw what was transpiring before his very eyes, he started yelling and running down the steps from the porch after them. "Hey, Cuz, what the hell y'all doing?"

As Keith's cousin and his girlfriend got into a fight, she would break loose for several seconds and run around the car parked in front of the house while screaming and crying frantically. Every time she got away from him, he caught up to her and start hitting her again.

In the meantime, Keith ran back up the stairs to go inside the house and get Shirley Ann and Ronnie. Keith believed that if his cousin wasn't listening to him, maybe he'd listen to Keith's parents. As Shirley Ann, Ronnie, and Keith came out to the porch, they couldn't believe their eyes! Keith's cousin and his girlfriend were still running around the car, screaming and yelling at each other, in some three feet of snow that had accumulated since the early afternoon. Shirley Ann and Ronnie ran off the porch to intervene in the violent scene that was unfolding in front of their eyes. Shirley Ann, in her gown and heels, and Ronnie, in his tuxedo and dress shoes, chased both their relative and his girlfriend around the car several times. Shirley almost caught him, grabbing his suit coat, but then slipped and fell into the snow. "Shirley!" Ronnie yelled. "Are you okay?"

"Hell no!" she replied. "Forget this sh—. Let those mother—s kill each other! Help get me up now and take me in the house!"

As Ronnie and Keith helped Shirley Ann up, the cousin stopped chasing his girlfriend long enough to go and see about Shirley Ann. "Ma!" he said. (He had called Shirley Ann and Ronnie *Ma* and *Pa* for as long as they could remember.) "I'm so sorry, Ma. I didn't mean to hurt you." Sobbing, he followed them all into the house.

Once inside, Ronnie, Keith, and the cousin sat Shirley Ann down on one of the chairs. Keith grabbed his cousin by the arm and said, "Come here!" he snapped. As Keith pulled him around the corner he said to him "What the hell got into you? What the hell was all that nonsense out there about, man?"

His cousin replied, "All that nonsense was about this . . . look!" Keith's cousin takes his right hand, slides it into the inside pocket of his suit coat and pulls out a beautiful silver box. "Man, I bought this three-karat diamond ring for thirty-seven hundred dollars before I left so I could come here and propose to her after your ceremony."

Keith, stunned, had no reply.

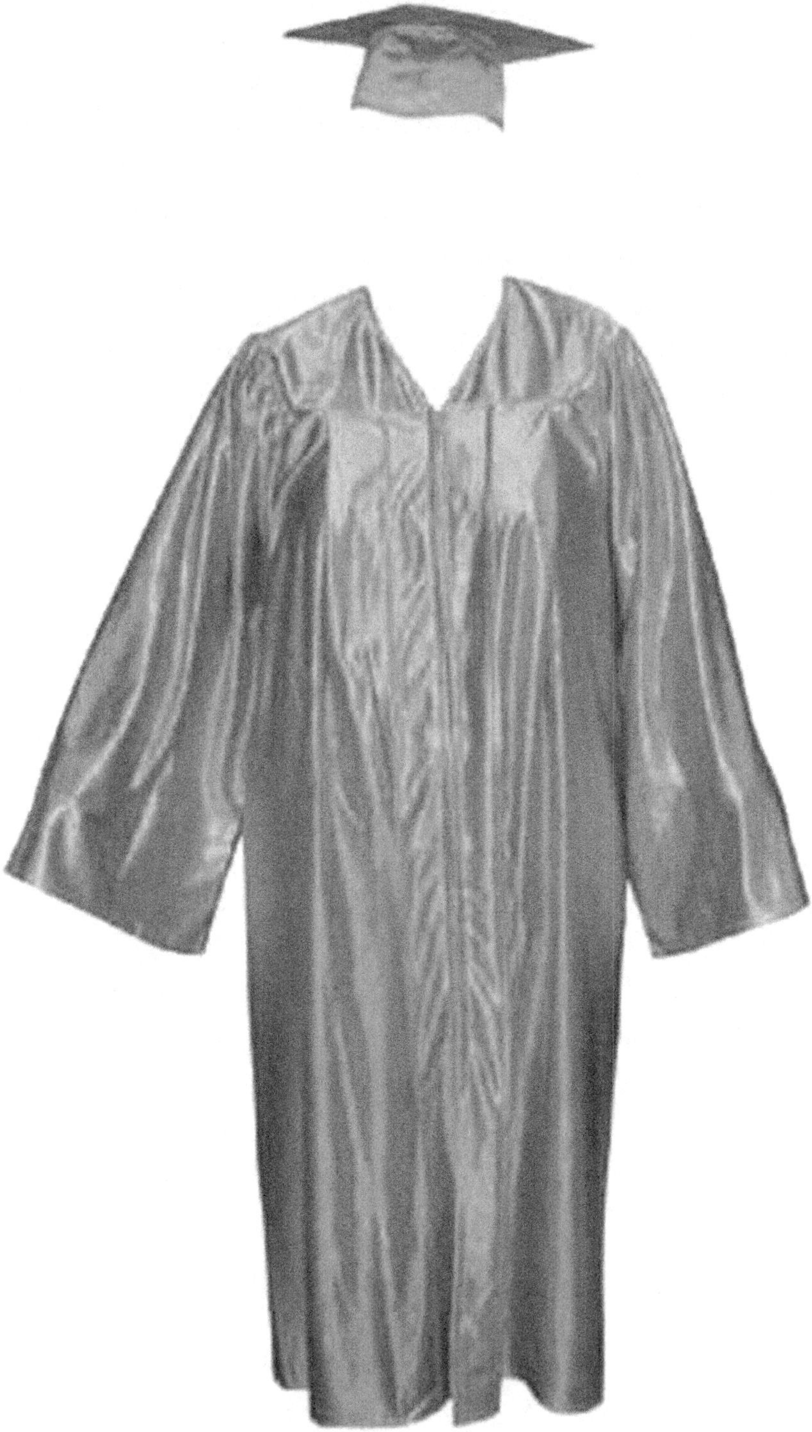

Part 9
1994

$\mathcal{S}$OME YEARS BACK, Karen had finally resolved to move out of Shirley Ann's and Ronnie's house. After looking around in several areas, she decided she could no longer waste any time looking for a place, so she could just move into the local housing project to start out. She realized now was as good a time as any to begin her life anew, away from Shirley Ann's and Ronnie's grasping.

Karen had decided she needed to do something more with her life, and at the tender age of thirty she enrolled in college for a degree in business management, and after seven years she finally graduated with her bachelor's degree in business. This was probably to her the toughest seven years in her life. She worked several jobs while putting herself through college, and being a single mother didn't make it any easier. With so many adversities to overcome the last few years, she persevered, and it paid off.

Karen at this point in her life had three children. She knew that being led by her feelings and not her gut instinct played a big part in her decisions. However, she was the kind of person who would chalk up her mistakes as a learning experience and move on with the next aspect of her life. Her daughter, Charla, was now in her late teens. Karen's two sons were three and thirteen years of age.

The youngest child Elijah's coming about was a surprise to everyone. Karen, while attending college, came across a couple of different men in her path. One character's name was Vincent Del Rey III. He believed he was God's gift to women everywhere. He lived his life daily to prove this fact to others as well as himself. What he didn't understand, if he was really all he claimed to be, was why he still resided in the house with his "mums" (as he often referred to his mother) at forty years of age. So when Karen established that, after his looks, there was not anything else there, she let him go his way and moved on.

The next character in her life was probably just as bad as Vincent, and he wasn't even one bit of handsome to behold. Frederick Lee was his name. Frederick was very intelligent and also a nontraditional student. Karen, being a trusting person, was easily sucked in by his intellect. They started seeing each other and soon became serious. Several months went by, and one night she decided to pay Frederick a visit. She had just been to the doctor's office and was told she was expecting. Karen was riveted with fear for some reason, so she decided to tell Frederick that evening.

As she pulled into his driveway, she noticed another car besides his in the driveway. She also noticed the blinds were not closed at this time of night. She decided to quietly walk up to the house and see what was going on. As she approached the house, she peeked into the living room window and discovered Frederick and another woman smoking on what she thought was a funny-looking pipe. Karen was so shocked that she decided never to see Frederick again. She thought it would be better to just have the baby and go on with her life, so that was what she did. She finished her last couple years of college and graduated in the spring of '94.

The day of Karen's graduation was filled with excitement and emotion for her. She scrambled to get everything together the night before. She wanted to get a final count of how many of her family would be attending this important occasion. "Ma and Dad!" she said excitedly as she looked in the mirror while trying on her graduation gown. "You know you have to be at the ceremony one hour early to get a good seat!"

Shirley Ann replied, "Uh, Karen, your dad and I won't be able to make it to your graduation."

"Why not?"

"Well, I'm not feeling well, and your dad, he can't go without me," Shirley Ann said with no emotion.

"What!" Karen exclaimed. "You mean to tell me that after seven years of me attending college, my own parents decided out of the blue not to come to my graduation." She wiped away a tear.

"We having a damn party for you afterward! What more do you want from us?" Shirley screamed.

"Karen!" Ronnie said. "We are sorry, but we will be here when you get back."

As Karen walked away, blinking back tears, she tried to control her emotions still. She could not believe that only her sister and children were attending her graduation.

As she prepared herself for commencement the next day, she reminisced about all the situations she had overcome the last few years to finally get here. She decided that if she could endure them all, she could make it through her graduation alone . . . without her family.

Part 10
1996

*C*HARLES WAS NOW about forty and married. He met a woman from his job, and they tied the knot after dating about two years. Now Charles always wanted a family with children, seeing how he had helped rear Karen's, Dee's, and Ronnell's children as if he were their father. Unfortunately, what Charles longed for did not come to pass. The woman he married, Darlene, had two sons; one was an adult by then, and the other was nine years old. The two boys were rather rough around the edges and lacked proper guidance in a lot of areas because of their upbringing. Darlene for many years was a single mom who had to be out of the house working two jobs just to make ends meet. They were latchkey kids for the most part. This left them lots of time to get into mischief and succumb to peer pressure.

Now Charles, with a clear idea of what a family should be about, came to the reality very quickly: the fantasy of being the kind of dad to go outside and throw the football around with his new son pretty much wasn't going to happen at this point in time. He deemed that to be true the very first time he encountered the younger son, Willie. Charles, always polite, mild-mannered, and cordial, decided to break the ice with the young boy and start up a conversation during Darlene's and his first date. He was sitting in the dining room with Willie while waiting for her to get dressed and said, "So how do you like school?"

Willie looked up at Charles and replied, "Why do you want to know? You ain't my daddy!"

"I'm not trying to be your daddy, young man. I'm just trying to strike up a conversation with you."

Just as Willie was about to reply, Darlene came from getting dressed and said, "I'm ready!"

As Charles stood, he replied to Darlene, "I'm ready too!" Then he walked past Willie with a disappointed glare. Charles thought upon that evening and hoped that it would not be the norm for his and Willie's relationship. But as the relationship between Charles and Darlene grew, so did the tension and resentment between Charles and Willie.

After Charles and Darlene married, the pressures of the stepdad-stepson relationship adjustment period really took its toll on Charles. He felt like there could never be any open avenue of communication between Willie and himself. Willie was getting older and more disruptive to his family as well as others. Being easily influenced by negative factors, Willie was always determined to go against the grain. Charles did everything in his power to enter into a king of parental role that he'd desired all his life to have. The irony of the whole situation was that, although he desired to be the dad Willie needed, the only role he could really take for Willie in reality was at the opposite end of the spectrum. Charles was the model father, especially to his nieces and nephews. However, he would never get the chance to know the complete pleasure of being the caring father because Willie wouldn't let him.

This factor also caused some grievances within Charles and Darlene's relationship as well. They would often spat about Willie and his downward spiraling behavior. Darlene thought Charles could be more understanding, whereas Charles thought Darlene was in complete denial when it came to Willie. Whatever the case was, Charles decided to hang in there and just take one day at a time.

Several years went by, and Willie grew older; all too soon, he was sixteen years of age. Willie had unfortunately followed in his brother's footsteps and become a menace to society. Stealing cars, drinking, and smoking marijuana were his vices. Some people acknowledged he might even be responsible for a couple of neighborhood drive-by shootings. Charles had pretty much at this point in time washed his hands of Willie.

Darlene, on the other hand, still tried to make excuses for his behavior. It got to the point that Darlene was Willie's enabler. She spent much of her time worrying about Willie and not spending enough time paying attention to Charles.

One day, as Charles was washing his car in the backyard of the yellow house, he noticed a police cruiser with two officers inside pulled in right behind his car. As they got out and started walking to the back toward him, Charles felt a tight knot in his stomach telling him that something wasn't quite right. "Hello, officers!" Charles said.

"Hello," they replied.

"We are trying to locate a Willie Hudson," the first officer said. "Would you know who that is, and where can we locate him?"

"Well, officer, he is my stepson, but I have no idea where he is," Charles replied. "You see he has become a big problem for his mother and me. So we kicked him out about two weeks ago."

The officer said, "Well, sir, I'm sorry to inform you that when we find him he will be prosecuted to the fullest extent of the law. We have reason to believe he robbed some customers at the drive-thru a little while ago. When we find him—and we will—he will be put into the juvenile justice center until he reaches twenty-one years of age."

As Charles listened to the officers, the uncomfortable feeling he initially felt soon changed to a feeling of relief.

Part II
1998

KELVIN NEVER MARRIED Linda. They broke up shortly after they got back home from visiting his family years before. Kelvin believed the struggles they would have to go through, because of being an interracial couple, would not work out for him in the long run.

Several months later he met a young lady who was also in the service and courted her for a while. They married, had two children, and reared them together up until the children were in their late teens. Because of unresolved issues and the hurt Kelvin so often felt in his life, he turned to certain things to comfort him. Unfortunately he would find comfort in friends like Jack Daniels and Johnny Walker.

No matter how much he tried, Kelvin found those things to be more beneficial to him than any other relationship ever could be. Kelvin still held bitter emotions concerning his upbringing. Just the past, period, caused him a lot of hurt. Whether it had more to do with Shirley Ann's and Ronnie's rearing, his relationship with his twin brother, or maybe something happening while he was in the armed services as the source of all the alienated feelings, no one actually knew. What was clear was his lack of connection with most people in his life. Kelvin seemed to be neither a realist nor a dreamer but somewhere caught in the middle. However, the middle was all right with Kelvin.

On the other hand, for his wife and children it proved to be too much. His wife decided to separate from him and go her own way because his drinking was something that she could not fix by herself. She needed Kelvin to own up to the fact that he needed help. Since he could not, it was out of her hands.

He soon was deployed overseas, and that made his issues worse. Kelvin found that overseas it was free rein. The lifestyle was uninhibited and laid back. He could get as much as he wanted whenever he wanted. Any and everything was at his disposal—especially the alcohol.

Part 12
2000

SHIRLEY ANN AND Ronnie were getting older. Ronnie decided to retire from his job at the mill and enjoy the rest of his life. In the last several years he had gone through a spiritual transformation and become a God-fearing man. While Shirley Ann welcomed this transformation, she was still in the process of going through her own. She was now a faithful member of her church. Ronnie played the saxophone there and also sat on the deacon board. Ronnie's great grandmother had helped to build the church. He always thought it was a family tradition for them to maintain membership there.

Shirley Ann's health in the last couple of years was starting to decline. She was an avid smoker for many years and had no inclination to stop, until she was diagnosed with the beginning stages of emphysema. She immediately quit smoking, but unfortunately the damage was already done. Shirley Ann now became emotionally codependent on everyone around her more now than ever. She developed a mental and emotional dependency that sometimes would drive the rest of the family mad.

Ronnie had a tendency to play right into the hands of Shirley Ann, and now since he had somewhat mellowed out in his later age, it was proven to be even more to Shirley Ann's advantage. In spite of Shirley Ann's health, she was still able to maneuver people around to her way.

One day Shirley Ann went to the doctor's office. When she returned, she decided to tell everyone in her family that the doctor had instructed her she could no longer be by herself. Now the family had already come to the conclusion that this might be a somewhat exaggerated, fabricated tale. They had talked to the doctor, but if Shirley Ann wanted to play manipulation games, they would oblige her for a little while. Not to say that Shirley Ann was not sick, but it was not as extreme as she wanted to portray. Sometimes her manipulation tactics would overshadow her ailment. How then could anyone help her if she couldn't lay everything out on the line and be genuine? This was the ongoing dilemma in the family of how bad Shirley Ann really was.

It was the late sixties when Shirley Ann and Ronnie first moved into their yellow house with the blue fire hydrant. They were living in one of the local housing projects and scraped up enough money to put a down payment on their dream house. The one thing about the house they loved so much was that it was big and roomy. The house had a basement, living room, kitchen, dining room, and four bedrooms. It also had an attic with a sitting room and two more bedrooms. Therefore when Shirley Ann and Ronnie moved out of the projects, they decided to have their next-door neighbor (whose name was Shirley also) move into the house with them along with her mentally-challenged son Leonard.

Shirley Ann and Ronnie had befriended Shirley and Leonard while living in the projects and very soon became like family to them. People often would refer to Shirley and Shirley Ann as "Big Shirl" and "Little Shirl"—"Big Shirl" being Leonard's mom and "Little Shirl" being Shirley Ann. The only real family that Shirley and Leonard were accustomed to was Shirley Ann and Ronnie. So Shirl and Leonard moved into the attic of the house, and it became theirs. Shirl helped cook and clean and helped raise the children.

At one time the yellow house with the blue fire hydrant had accommodated fourteen people. Shirley Ann and Ronnie were two. Their children Ronnell, Charles, Kelvin, Keith, Karen, and Denise made it eight. Karen and Ronnell had two children apiece, which brought it to twelve. With Shirl and Leonard, the house held a grand total of fourteen people.

Now Shirley Ann and Ronnie were used to having everyone around until the tides of change blew in. First came Ronnell's accident. Then Kelvin went into the service. Denise got married. Karen moved out. Keith and Charles got married. The last people who were left with Shirley Ann and Ronnie were Shirl and Leonard.

After thirty-plus years of living in the yellow house, one day Shirl came home and said, "Hey, Shirley Ann, my cousin and his wife are moving, and I'm thinkin' 'bout takin' their house. Leonard and I should try to get our own now. I'm too old now to be not havin' my own."

Shirley Ann was reading the newspaper, bobbing over her bifocals. As soon as she heard Shirl speak, she looked up, disturbed, and replied, "Is this how you repay us for letting you stay here for all those years? You know we didn't have to let ya!"

Shirl said, "Shirley Ann, I thank you for all you and Ronnie did for me and Leonard, but we got to leave now. You have been the only family we've known, and that's something that I won't never forget."

As Shirley listened, she felt she was abandoned. Everyone who had ever lived in the house was now gone. She never imagined it would ever just be her and Ronnie. Neither did she ever want it to be.

Part 13
2002

*N*ow Keith was separated from Rita and was looking for some refuge.

He decided to ask his niece, Karen's daughter Charla, if he could stay there for a little while along with Charla's husband and their toddler. Charla agreed, and he soon moved in. Keith was for the most part no trouble at all. He worked most evenings and slept most days, so having Keith reside in the house was perfectly fine with them.

After about two years of Keith staying with his niece, Charla's husband received a job offer down in New Orleans. She and her husband decided that since Karen, Charla's mom, had moved away to Mississippi, they would be closer to her. Charla discussed plans about selling the house with her uncle Keith. Keith suggested that instead of selling the house, they might just let him stay there and take care of it; in case it didn't work out in New Orleans there would be a house to come back to. So it was agreed to let Keith sill reside there after Charla and her family left.

Keith, unfortunately, was still easily influenced by peers even later in life. Although he had made somewhat of a change, Keith never did have the most morally sound friends. He was employed by one of the best companies in the state, but he still decided to pursue other alternatives like being a street pharmacist. For some reason this appealed to Keith, who always struggled with prestige and power issues. He saw the glitz and glitter of it all, and that was what he desired.

So after Charla and her family moved, Keith decided to reinvent himself. He started having many acquaintances revolve in and out of the house. Many were derived from illegal activities. But to Keith this was what life was about.

Charla lived in New Orleans for two years. She separated from her husband and came back to the city. Now on her way from the bus station, her cousin Michael picked her up and said, "Hey, Cuz, it's good to have you back."

"It's good to be back!" she said. "Now the first thing I want to see is my house."

Michael replied, "Ummmm . . . about that. I don't think you should go to your house."

She smiled at him and said, "Quit playing!"

Michael said reluctantly, "I'm not playing!"

The smile on her face soon faded as she looked at him and said, "What's going on, Michael? Why can't I go to my house?"

"Because Keith has turned your house into a drug house, and I don't think it's safe for you and your child to stay there."

"What?" As Charla sat there in shock, she thought maybe Michael had something mixed up. Maybe he wasn't really saying what came out of his mouth. But she knew that if anyone about town knew anything of what was going on, it would be Michael. He knew the ins and outs of every situation about town, whether good or bad. So after processing in her head all this new information, Charla pretty much believed his information to be true indeed.

Upon arriving at the yellow house with the blue fire hydrant in front of it, still reeling from the news of the hour, Charla greeted her grandparents, Shirley Ann and Ronnie. Shirley Ann had cooked dinner and sat down to eat when she said, "So have you talked to your uncle Keith?"

"No, I have not," Charla stated.

Shirley Ann replied, "You know he really took care of the house for you all in the last few years while you were gone."

Charla interrupted, "You know, Grandma, I really don't want to talk about this right now."

"Talk about what?" Shirley Ann said.

"How my uncle is running amuck in my house, and if something happens, it's my responsibility . . . it will be on my head and not his!"

"What the hell are you talking about, Char?" Now Shirley Ann and Ronnie always had a way of turning their heads and not seeing what they really already knew: that their son might be up to something, not on the up-and-up. Keith took care of Shirley Ann and Ronnie by providing them with a bit of financial support. Shirley Ann and Ronnie were in their senior years now and on a fixed income. Any support that the children and grandchildren gave them was much welcomed—especially the extra help from Keith in the form of new doors, windows, flooring, and cupboards.

Charla chose not to play the game and get into the whole dilemma of the situation at hand. All she could see was that she was single, with a six-year-old and a child on the way and no place to live. The living quarters that she had entrusted to her uncle Keith for this very reason were unsafe and unfit.

Charla decided that after Labor Day weekend, she would make the effort to get Keith out of her house before something tragic happened.

Soon the annual family Labor Day barbecue and get-together at the big yellow house was under way. The day was relaxing until the inevitable reared its ugly head. Shirley Ann had been looking for Keith all day long. He promised her as usual he would be over to help, but he never made it. Keith stated to Shirley Ann later that he was tied up with other things and would make it over as soon as possible.

At eight in the evening Shirley Ann and other family members were cleaning up from the earlier picnic. Everyone started to pack up and go to their destinations. Shortly after everyone departed, the telephone rang. It was Michael (the cousin). "Hey, Ma!" He often referred to Shirley Ann as "Ma." "I think something happened to Keith!"

"What do you mean *something*?" Shirley Ann exclaimed.

"Well, I'm not sure if it was him . . . but it might be. I was told that someone with a silver Cadillac like the one he owns got shot—but it's two more guys I know myself with a silver Cadillac like his, so I'm not sure!"

Now it was public knowledge that Keith had a silver Cadillac. When Keith bought his car, two other younger guys who looked up to Keith bought the same car; thus the confusion whether the person who'd been shot was actually Keith! "Michael," Shirley yelled, "you have to give me more damn information . . . I don't know what to do! What am I supposed to do?"

"Ma!" Michael said. "My boy called me and told me this. He said he would find out and call me back."

Shirley Ann answered, "Michael, call me back right away."

"Wait!" Michael said. "Someone is on the other line." As Shirley Ann kept hold on the other line she felt a lump in her throat anticipating negative news. "Ma! My boy said it was him, and he's been shot six times in front of Charla's house!"

Shirley Ann dropped the phone from her ear and fell to the floor, yelling and screaming in tears.

Part 14
2004

*K*AREN AT THIS point in life had been married to a minister for about ten years. His name was Phillip. After she had Elijah, she met Phillip through a mutual friend. They were a perfect match, each giving what the other had needed, which was love, respect, and mutual admiration. People always observed that they complimented each other very well. Karen had finally found peace of mind when it came to love.

Karen also became a teacher and worked in the school system for many years. Her skills as a teacher came in handy when it came to Elijah also. Two years after Elijah was born, he was found to be autistic but highly functional. The doctors told Karen that he would suffer somewhat socially with his form of autism more than anything else. She decided to mainstream Elijah in the school system thereby keeping him in regular classes. She vowed that each school that he would go to was where she would teach in an effort to let him be as "normal" as possible.

She soon began to see the effects of his disease socially. Elijah had a hard time making friends, and because of this, he attached himself to Karen. Karen sought several doctors and specialists about this form of autism. But to no avail; no physician had any better solutions than she did.

Karen put off getting her master's in teaching because of Elijah's condition. She was convinced his needs far outweighed any of her wants and allowed herself to be at Elijah's disposal. Not having a master's in the state where she lived at times proved to be difficult.

Living in a new state came as a kind of culture shock to Karen at first. From the insects to the food, every aspect of it at first was just different for Karen, who had been a northerner all her life. Although she was ready and accepting of all possibilities, she fully understood this would be an adjustment for her. At times one of the biggest adjustments was the people.

She discovered there was nothing like southern hospitality, but she also discovered something she completely didn't realize living up north. Because of the economic factor in the state, the education process was structured completely different in this area of the country. Karen found out that unlike the school systems she had been accustomed to, in this area the funding that was usually generated directly to a specific school district for learning-disabled or special-needs children goes directly to the parent or guardian. Karen believed this left everyone a prisoner of the process. She saw firsthand that, because of the poverty in the area, parents would often opt for the funding instead of the chance for their child to be put in regular classes. She talked to her family about several of these instances. Karen herself discussed with the students' families she taught about placement in regular classes. Most parents decided against it for the sake of the extra income. Seeing this, she decided never to put Elijah in this situation and to keep him "mainstreamed" in the school system.

Elijah did have his problems, but they worked through them, taking one day at a time.

Part 15
2006

The year 2006 found Shirley Ann's and Ronnie's clan in several different pathways. Shirley Ann herself was admitted into a nursing home for COPD. Although she is in long-term extended care now, she is still up with all the goings-on. She still has her family constantly at the nursing home seeing about her. Although she cannot speak because of the ventilator, she writes to them on notebook paper. Unfortunately, a couple of years later she ended up succumbing to her disease and passed away. This devastated the family the strong spirited, tough-natured matriarch of the family was now gone forever. The legacy she left along with her fighting spirit, encompassed her family for the rest of their lives. Shirley Ann would be forever loved and remembered for her life's sacrifice she made in an attempt to keep her family together.

Ronnie still stood by Shirley Ann and was constantly with her at the nursing home. Ronnie sat there with Shirley Ann for several hours daily. Ronnie, who loved Shirley Ann very much, unfortunately never had the chance of taking control of certain aspects in life. He found that doing simple things like paying the bills and balancing the checkbook overwhelmed him after Shirley Ann went into the nursing home. He had to learn all the things he had hung back from before because of Shirley Ann's abundant strength in earlier years.

Ronnie still somehow managed to find time to play a gig every now and then. Although he still had it in him, his gigs were far and few between. He was also honored by the state's University music and jazz departments for his life long accomplishments in the arts. His achievements ceremony was marked with senators, congressmen and family who all enjoyed his musical contributions over the years.

Denise at this point in her life had found her Prince Charming, although she decided to "wait and see" when it came down to the nuptials. She had met a nice guy several years earlier, and they had been dating for quite some time. Denise, although very much in love with this man, felt apprehensive because of her past track record concerning love. Past experiences left her with a distaste regarding marriage. However, Denise finally took the leap of faith and had a beautiful Vegas wedding in the summertime. She was now truly experiencing her happily ever after.

Keith's destructive behavior caught up to him. He was sentenced to two years for drugs. His decisions cost him everything including his freedom. His materialistic nature led to a severe downfall. He became a prisoner of his own mind-set long before he was ever sentenced.

As for Kelvin he was determined to prove he could live by his own rules and survive the odds. In any other sort of life this would have been good, but not in his situation. After years of living in Germany, Kelvin became a functioning alcoholic. He could hold down employment but just could not stop the daily surge of alcohol consumption. His uncontrollable habit just became the normal routine for him. Although anyone who knew him could see that when he was not incapacitated his heart was bigger than most. Kelvin's denial of his sickness made him create walls and continue a pattern of having many broken relationships.

Charles, always the level-headed child, took a more even route in life in his pursuit of individualism by steering away from any negatives and staying more positive. Unfortunately, he never had any children of his own. He did, however, prove himself to be a positive role model in the life of his nieces and nephews. He was much appreciated by them for his dedication. Every Father's Day he was sure to receive a token of love from them.

Karen finally found love and happiness with the minister from out of state. She would say they were meant to be together. Karen learned that sometimes you have to kiss a couple of frogs before you kiss your prince!

And as for the big yellow house with the blue fire hydrant in front of it . . . it's still standing in one piece, although there is not much life in it anymore. Every now and then you can find someone coming or going from the house. The love and lessons of triumphs and trials learned in this house affected each life in a positive or negative way. Ultimately no matter what, Shirley Ann and Ronnie taught a valuable lesson to the family as a whole. Family is the bond that will never be broken. The only thing that really matters when it all boils down is the legacy of who you loved and who loved you in the end. Family is truly forever. All in all, it's pretty much quiet at the house now. However, if only the walls could talk!

About the Author

*D*ANICA HOBBS IS a writer and spoken-word poetess. She was given a gift to write at a very young age. Her talents and gift have now brought her to complete her very first book, *The Yellow Legacies*, a compilation of short stories about life, love, and family.

About the Book

I AM VERY GLAD that people are enjoying *The Yellow Legacies*. This was a labor of love that I wrote in 2006. It is loosely based on experiences that I encountered in the house where I grew up. It is about love, life, and lessons but most of all family. It is about fears and tears and overcoming the past. It is ultimately about the wonderful family I have always truly appreciated, loved, and admired from those moments while growing up to even now.

Made in the USA
Coppell, TX
15 April 2022